Learn About Books

Whales and Sharks

Written by
Bobbie Whitcombe

BRIMAX BOOKS • NEWMARKET • ENGLAND

The whale family includes the biggest animals that have ever lived. The largest ones are the **blue whales**. They are bigger than any dinosaurs. Whales live in the sea and the water holds up their enormous weight.

Whales are not fishes. They are mammals. They cannot breathe under water and they are warm-blooded. This means the blood in their bodies stays at a constant temperature.

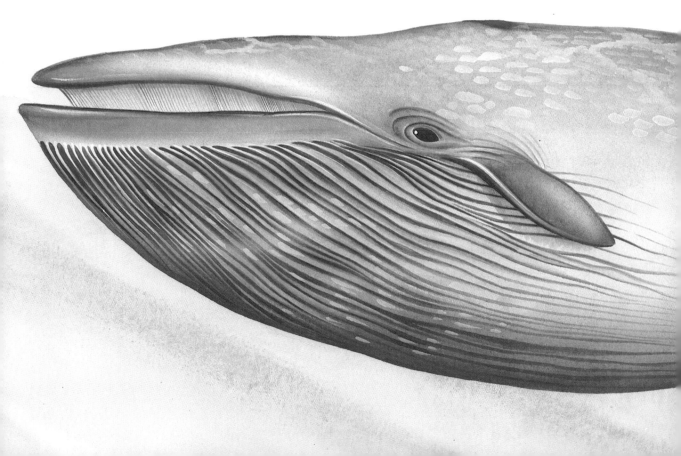

Dolphins and **porpoises** also belong to the whale family. They like to play in the water. These dolphins are following a ship.

Like us, whales use their lungs to breathe.
They have to come up to the surface
and blow out the air from their lungs.
This is called spouting.
Then they take in fresh
air and dive again.

This is a **sperm whale**
It is diving deep to
catch squid. It can stay under water
for a long time.

Some of the biggest whales have no teeth. They have a piece of horn in their mouths called baleen. They feed on tiny sea creatures called krill.

This **humpback whale** swims near the surface of the sea where there is plenty of krill. The whale opens its mouth wide and takes a huge gulp of water. Then it pushes out the water through the baleen, leaving the food behind.

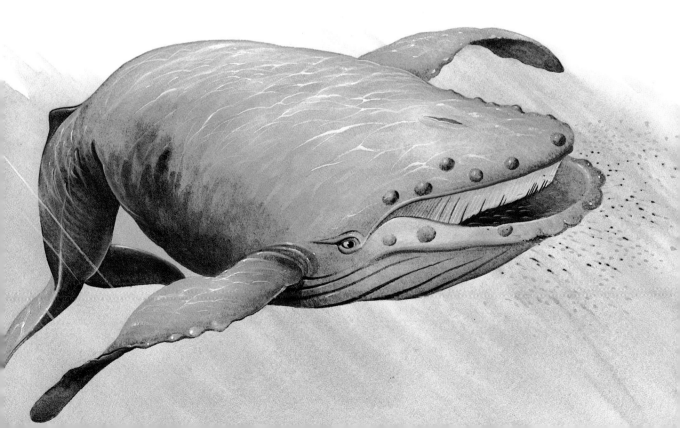

The **blue whale** is the biggest living
animal. It can weigh as much as 30
elephants. But its food is mainly krill.
It eats about 2,000 kg (4,400 pounds)
of krill each day.
The picture shows
what krill looks like
close up. They are
like shrimps. Each one
is about 5 cm (2 inches)
long.

krill

Some whales do have teeth.
They feed on squid and
fish. The **narwhal** is a
white whale with two teeth.
In the males, one of the
teeth grows into a long
tusk.

The **beluga** is also
a white whale but
it has over 32 teeth.
It lives in seas near
the North Pole.

Whale babies grow for about a year inside their mother. A whale has only one baby at a time. A baby whale is called a calf.

This **right whale** calf can drink its mother's milk under water. The calf stays close by its mother for about a year.

This baby **blue whale** has been born
under the water. Its mother pushes it
up to the surface as soon as it is born
so it can breathe. Another female will
swim nearby watching out for danger.

The **killer whale** has sharp teeth. It eats fish, squid, penguins and even seals. It can swim very fast. Sometimes killer whales leap right out of the water to swim faster.

Look at this **porpoise** leaping out of the water. Porpoises chase and dive for fish in coastal waters.

Dolphins are very clever. They can learn to do tricks like this. They sense things in the water by making high-pitched sounds. The echoes are bounced back by fish or other objects. This helps the dolphins find their prey.

Whales have thick layers of fat to keep the warmth in their bodies. This is called blubber. People have hunted whales for over a thousand years. They used blubber for oil to make candles and soap. They also used the baleen to stiffen ladies' corsets.

There are not many whales left now. They are still hunted today for meat and blubber. Some countries have laws to stop people killing whales. It is very sad that man is the worst enemy of these huge, gentle creatures.

Unlike whales, sharks
are fish, not mammals.
They breathe through
flaps behind the head
called gills. Some
sharks are as big
as a boat.

Many sharks look big and fierce but are
harmless to people. This **basking shark** has
no teeth. It floats on the water eating
tiny sea creatures called plankton.
Can you see its gills?

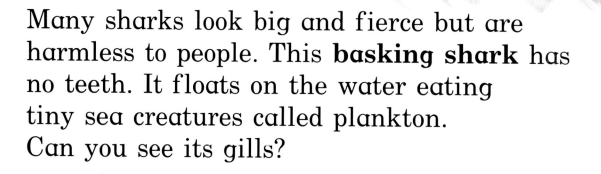

This **whale shark** is the largest fish in the world. It can be longer than a sailing ship. It also feeds on plankton and small fish.

The **dwarf shark** is the smallest of the sharks. It is no bigger than the mackerel shown above it.

This shark is dangerous!
It is the **great white
shark**. It eats seals,
fish and dolphins. It
will also attack people.
Look at its sharp teeth.

The **hammerhead shark** is
a vicious hunter and may
also attack people. It
has an eye at each end
of its hammer-shaped
head.

Look at the **wobbegong** hiding on the sea
bed. It pounces out on fish that pass
and feeds on them. It is also called a
carpet shark. It is dangerous because it
is hard to see among the rocks and weed.
A swimmer might get a nasty bite on the
foot. Wobbegongs live near the coast of
Australia.

Like other fish, some sharks lay eggs.
Others give birth to live babies. The
hammerhead has about 30 babies at once.
The babies grow inside their mother for
about two years. As soon as they are
born, the baby sharks swim off in search
of food. Unlike whales, they do not
need to stay with their mother.

All sharks are very fast swimmers. They
have long slim bodies and strong tail fins.
This helps them to move quickly through
the water. Sharks have a good sense of
smell. They can smell blood in the water
up to half a kilometre away. They will swim
swiftly towards it in the hope of food.
Sharks can be fast and fierce hunters.

Can you remember the names of these whales and sharks?

great white shark
blue whale

hammerhead shark
sperm whale